The truth is stranger than fiction… a story for Hannah,
Iola and Web and families all around the world – CB

For Jules, Ames and Els, with love – SW

For Jay, with love – AH

Brimming with creative inspiration, how-to projects, and useful information to enrich your everyday life, Quarto Knows is a favourite destination for those pursuing their interests and passions. Visit our site and dig deeper with our books into your area of interest: Quarto Creates, Quarto Cooks, Quarto Homes, Quarto Lives, Quarto Drives, Quarto Explores, Quarto Gifts, or Quarto Kids.

Inspiring | Educating | Creating | Entertaining

JANETTA OTTER-BARRY BOOKS

**The publishers and authors would like to thank
Dr Brian Rosen of The Natural History Museum, London
for his invaluable advice and support as science consultant for this book.**

Text © 2015 Catherine Barr and Steve Williams. Illustrations © 2015 Amy Husband.
First Published in 2015 by Frances Lincoln Children's Books,
an imprint of The Quarto Group.
The Old Brewery, 6 Blundell Street, London N7 9BH, United Kingdom.
T (0)20 7700 6700 F (0)20 7700 8066 www.QuartoKnows.com

First paperback edition published in 2018.
The right of Amy Husband to be identified as the illustrator and Catherine Barr and Steve Williams to be identified as the authors of this work has been asserted by them in accordance with the Copyright, Designs and Patents Act, 1988 (United Kingdom).

A catalogue record for this book is available from the British Library.

ISBN 978-1-84780-755-7

The illustrations were created with mixed media and collage.

Set in Gill Sans

Published by Janetta Otter-Barry
Designed by Judith Escreet

Manufactured in Guangdong, China [CC102017]

9 8 7 6 5 4 3 2 1

CATHERINE BARR studied Ecology and trained as a journalist. She worked at Greenpeace International for seven years as a wildlife and forestry campaigner and has a long-running interest in natural history and environmental issues. Working as an editor at the Natural History Museum, she researched and wrote two major summer exhibitions: *Dinosaurs of the Gobi Desert* and *Myths and Monsters*. She has also written *Elliot's Arctic Surprise*, a picture book about protecting the Arctic, published in 2015. She lives near Hay-on-Wye in Herefordshire with her partner and two daughters.

STEVE WILLIAMS is a chartered biologist with a degree in Marine Biology and Applied Zoology from the University of Wales. His lifelong love of wildlife was further inspired by eight years at sea, after which he trained as a teacher, and now teaches science in a rural comprehensive school in Wales. He is a keen beekeeper and astronomer, living beneath the dark skies of Hay-on-Wye with his wife and two daughters.

AMY HUSBAND studied Graphic Art at Liverpool School of Art. Her first picture book, *Dear Miss*, was winner of the Cambridgeshire Children's Picture Book Award in 2010. Amy lives in York with her partner, working in a studio with views of York Minster.

The Story of
LIFE

A first book about evolution

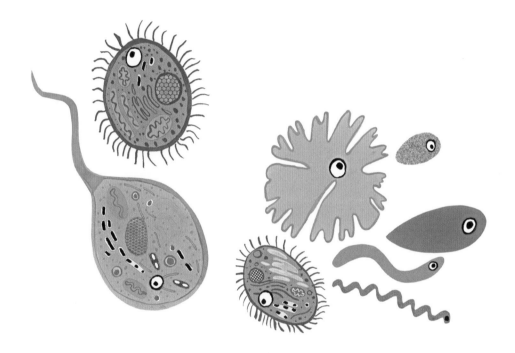

Catherine Barr and **Steve Williams**
Illustrated by **Amy Husband**

F

FRANCES LINCOLN
CHILDREN'S BOOKS

At first, **nothing** lived on Earth. It was a very hot and noisy place.

Choking gas exploded from volcanoes and oceans of lava bubbled around the globe.

Fountains of melting rock spattered burning land under clouds of ash.

volcano

lava

4.5 billion years ago

And massive rocks from space, called meteoroids, smashed into churning seas.

meteoroids

Deep underwater, hot black gases belched towards the surface of this strange, lifeless world.

Then, in the deep dark ocean,
something amazing happened.

In warm water, near underwater
volcanoes called black smokers,
some tiny floating bits came together.

black smokers

bubbles

3.5 billion years ago

These bits were so small that you couldn't possibly see them. They could have dropped from space or bubbled up from under the seabed.

They formed the beginning of life on Earth.

tiny bits

seabed

This first life
was just an incredibly small shapeless blob, called a cell.

first cell

As time passed cells lived together, making sticky, slimy mats that grew into mounds as big as pillows.

slimy mat of cells

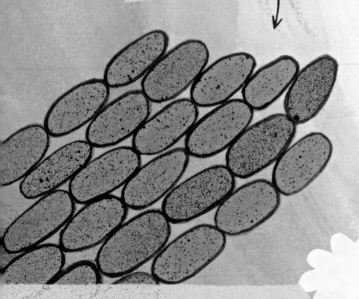

3 billion years ago

invisible oxygen

first continents

Some cells started using sunlight, water and a gas in the air, to help them grow.

Cells multiplied into billions. And so the seas clouded with lots of new kinds of life.

Some cells puffed out an invisible gas called oxygen, which completely changed the air and even the colour of the planet.

Circling the globe, the oxygen turned black rocks shades of yellow, red and brown.

invisible oxygen

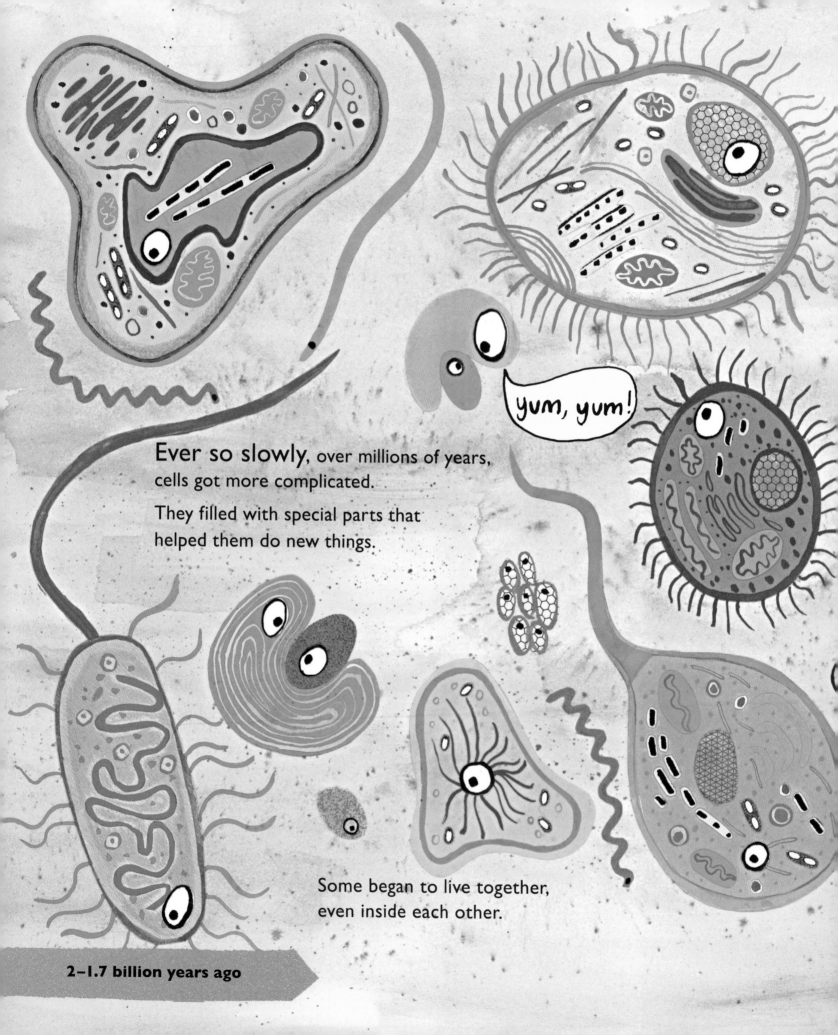

yum, yum!

Ever so slowly, over millions of years, cells got more complicated.

They filled with special parts that helped them do new things.

Some began to live together, even inside each other.

2–1.7 billion years ago

We are the world's first animals.

As the air filled with oxygen, some cells began to use it to grow and grow. So this new gas changed living things for ever.

Cells grew into all kinds of weird and wonderful shapes and sizes. Some of these became the first animals. And life on Earth really began to get going.

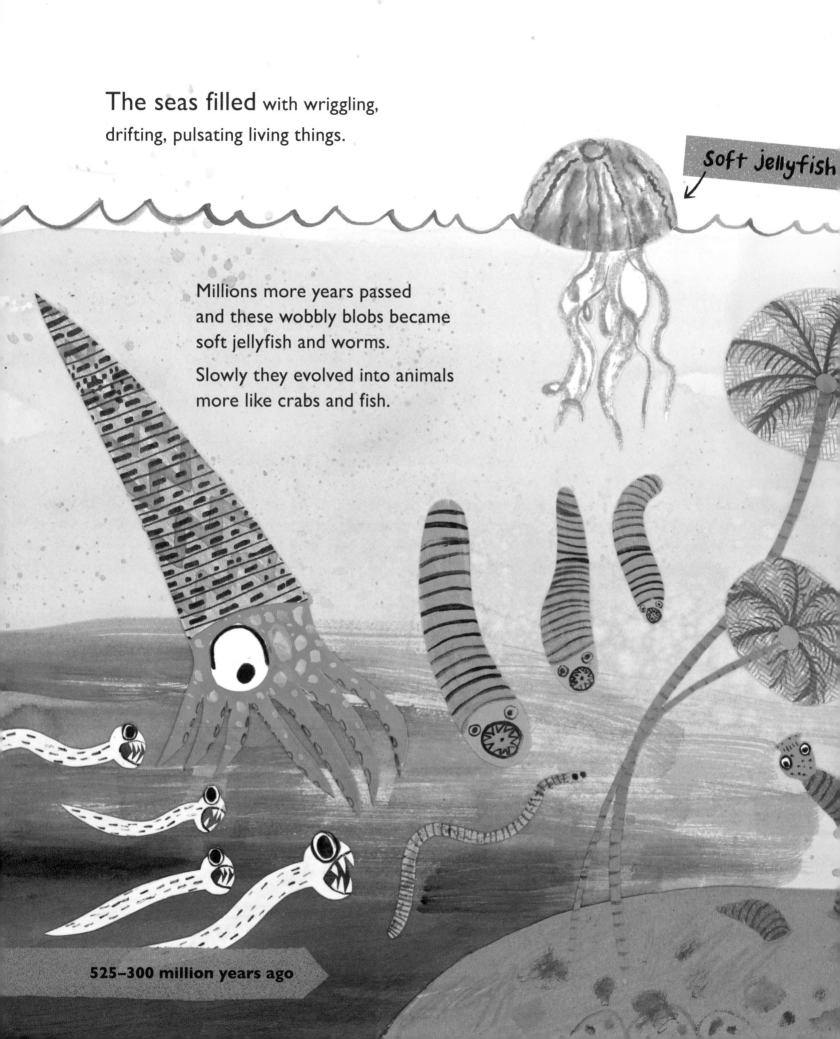

The seas filled with wriggling, drifting, pulsating living things.

Millions more years passed and these wobbly blobs became soft jellyfish and worms.

Slowly they evolved into animals more like crabs and fish.

Soft jellyfish

525–300 million years ago

Some of these sea creatures fought for space, ate each other and grew bigger and bigger.

Others nibbled plants and gobbled the remains of dead animals drifting by.

Mmmm DINNER

even bigger fish

Trilobite

worms

bigger fish

little fish

From the dark depths to the shallow pools, different types of creatures found different wet and watery places to live.

With the seas full of life,

plants and animals finally began to invade the land.

In shallow waters, soggy weeds stretched towards the sun – very, very slowly evolving into tall trees. Different plants appeared, spreading hundreds of shades of green across the land.

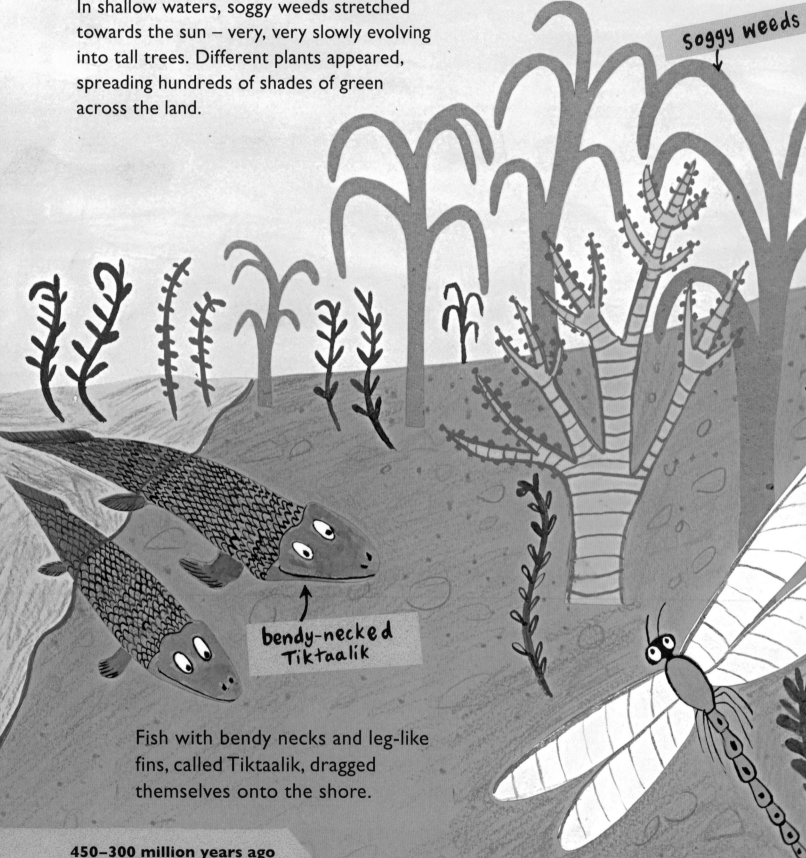

Soggy weeds

bendy-necked Tiktaalik

Fish with bendy necks and leg-like fins, called Tiktaalik, dragged themselves onto the shore.

450–300 million years ago

tall trees

Eventually swampy forests filled with frog-like creatures and other slimy things.

Giant insects took off and flew for the first time, through hot, damp air.

Lovely and squelchy in here!

clouds of dus[t]

Then disaster struck – something terrible happened that killed most life on Earth.

We don't know what it was and scientists are still hunting for clues.

Perhaps massive clouds of dust from exploding volcanoes blocked out the sun.

250 million years ago

dinosaur footprints

Without light or heat it was hard to survive.
But scaly lizard-like animals did survive.
They laid the first eggs out of water,
began to multiply and grow bigger than ever before.

In time, they became the most enormous creatures
that have ever lived on land — the dinosaurs.

Where is everybody?

first eggs with shells

When the largest dinosaurs walked, the Earth shook. These gigantic reptiles thundered across deserts, while others waded through swamps.

Tyrannosaurus Rex

As tall as a house, with jagged teeth, some were truly terrifying.

Brachiosaurus

230–200 million years ago

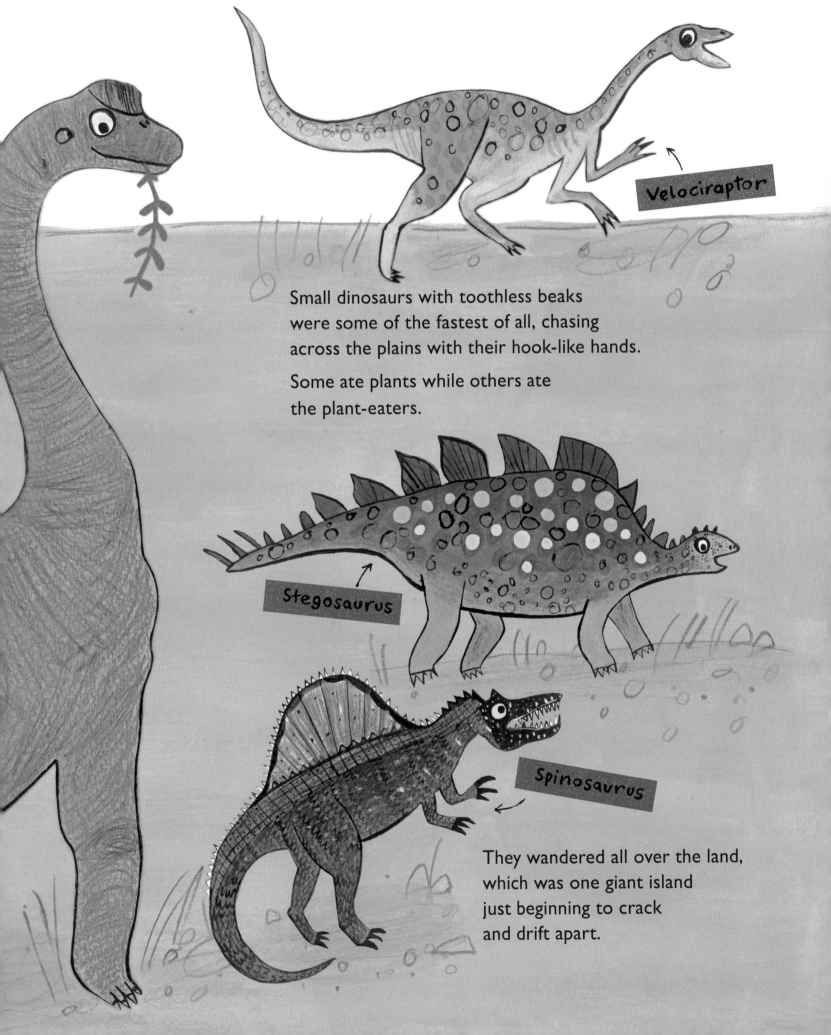

Velociraptor

Small dinosaurs with toothless beaks
were some of the fastest of all, chasing
across the plains with their hook-like hands.

Some ate plants while others ate
the plant-eaters.

Stegosaurus

Spinosaurus

They wandered all over the land,
which was one giant island
just beginning to crack
and drift apart.

Extraordinary lizard-like creatures cruised through the air, while huge crocodiles, sharks and other giant reptiles swam in warm seas.

The air, land and sea filled with millions of different plants and animals.

Pterodactyls

Ichthyosaur

Shark

Pliosaur

200–65 million years ago

Little furry animals, the first mammals, scuttled into holes in crowded forests.

They were the first to have babies rather than lay eggs.

All kinds of living things fought for food and space.

The most successful survived, and the first birds began to squawk and sing.

Splashes of colour appeared
as the first flowers warmed in the sun.

With the help of insects, these flowers
thrived and spread – their new scents
drifting on the breeze.

144–65 million years ago

But once more, everything was about to change.

meteorite

A gigantic rock, called a meteorite, crashed into the planet – blasting thick dust into the air.

Volcanoes erupted around the globe.

Living things were smothered as dust settled, lava flowed and temperatures fell.

Magnolias

The world was plunged into icy darkness.
In freezing weather, without food,
the dinosaurs died.

65–10 million years ago

This time, the little hairy animals survived.
Perhaps they found shelter and their fur kept them warm.

These warm-blooded, furry creatures evolved into
lots of different kinds of animals.

And so, with the dinosaurs gone, the mammals
took over the world.

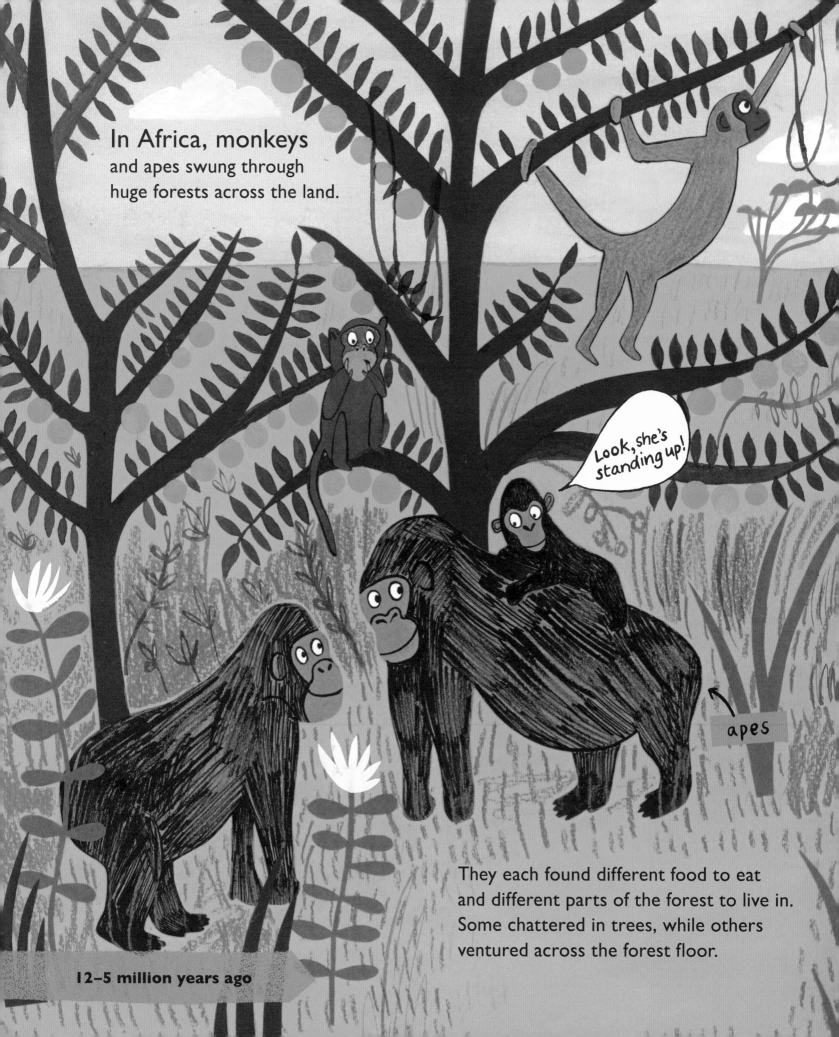

monkeys

Over time, less rain fell and forests became
more patchy. Apes that started using just two
legs to cross more open land, survived better.

They evolved into the first humans.

Lucy

Scientists found the bones of one of these first ape-like humans, and they called her Lucy.

Lucy lived over three million years ago.

They learned to make fire to keep warm.

They sharpened stones for tools, and they hunted.

stone tool

5 million–60,000 years ago

Fossil footprints show that these early people walked side by side across the open plains.

hunting spear

Different groups began to walk out of Africa and find new places to live.

As they explored, the Earth got colder and colder, ice spread and the seas froze.

In these ice ages, life for early people was a real struggle.

The people who used tools and found ways to keep warm survived better. These people spread and settled all over the world.

Their brains developed and they began to think more like us.

60,000 years ago—today

As the Earth warmed, they started farming and growing food.

Everyone in the world is related to these survivors, including you.

People, like all life on Earth,
will carry on evolving over time.
We are learning more and more
about the world around us.

today

Yet we are destroying wild places and changing the climate.
And so humans are causing the extinction of many plants and animals.

But like all living things, we depend on each other to survive.
The challenge for all of us is to care for this blue-green planet
that is our home.

With or without us, our planet will spin through
space for billions of years to come.

So the end of this book is far from the end
of the incredible story of life on Earth.

What next?

today

60,000 years ago–today

Glossary of useful words

Black smoker – an undersea volcano that spurts out super-hot water full of tiny black bits – making it look like black smoke.

Cells – tiny living things that are the building blocks of all life on Earth.

Continent – an enormous area of land. Today there are seven continents.

Dinosaurs – reptiles, often huge, which lived on Earth over 65 million years ago.

Evolution – the way in which living things change over time, sometimes into new kinds of life.

Extinct – living things that have died out, and no longer exist on Earth.

Fossil – evidence found in the rocks, of living things that existed millions of years ago.

Ice ages – long periods of time when ice covered large parts of the Earth.

Lava – red-hot, melted rock that erupts from a volcano.

Lucy – the name given to the fossil of one of the first ape-like humans found in Africa.

Mammals – warm-blooded, hairy animals that give birth to living young and feed their babies with milk that they produce.

Meteorite – a rock that has travelled through space and crashed into the Earth.

Meteoroid – a rock travelling through space.

Oxygen – a gas with no colour or smell that is made by plants. Most living things need to breathe oxygen to stay alive.

Photosynthesis – the way that plants use sunlight, water and a gas called carbon dioxide to help them grow.

Reptiles – cold-blooded animals with tough skin that lay eggs on land.

Tiktaalik – a large fish with four leg-like fins that was one of the first creatures to crawl out of water and walk on land. It is extinct.

Trilobite – an extinct sea creature that had a tough skeleton on the outside of its body, divided into three parts. It lived over 250 million years ago.

Volcano – a mountain or a hill with a large opening, called a crater, through which lava and gases erupt from the Earth's crust.

ALSO IN THE SERIES FROM FRANCES LINCOLN CHILDREN'S BOOKS

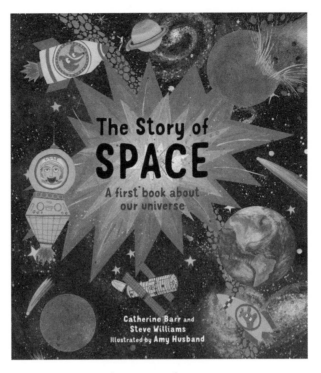

The Story of Space

Written by Catherine Barr and Steve Williams
Illustrated by Amy Husband

ISBN: 978-1-84780-748-9

Before the Big Bang, there was NOTHING AT ALL. No galaxies, no stars,
no planets and no life. No time, no space, no light and no sound. Then, suddenly,
13.8 billion years ago, IT ALL BEGAN...

This story of our universe is beautifully illustrated for younger children. Travel back in
time to the Big Bang, see galaxies and stars form, join the first man on the moon, and
wonder what mysteries are still waiting to be discovered...

'Ably straddling the divide between humour and wonder. With its accessible
text and welcoming design, this is a perfect book for the young space-farer' - *The Guardian*

Frances Lincoln titles are available from all good bookshops.
You can also buy books and find out more about your favourite titles,
authors and illustrators on our website: www.franceslincoln.com